Shasta's Second Chance

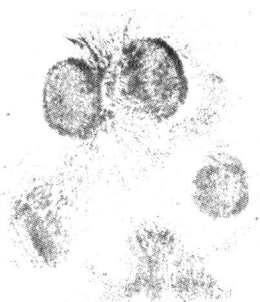

Lindsey Kitchen

SHASTA

ISBN: 978-0-615-37620-2

Acknowledgements:

Thanks to everyone that helped bring this book to life, reading, rereading, and editing. We couldn't have done it without you.

Thanks also to petfinder.com through which I found my best girl Shasta, and she found her forever home.

Shasta's Second Chance

Table of Contents

This book is dedicated to my husband and Shasta's pal Tim Butch who translated it from its original handwritten chicken scratch to something more readable.

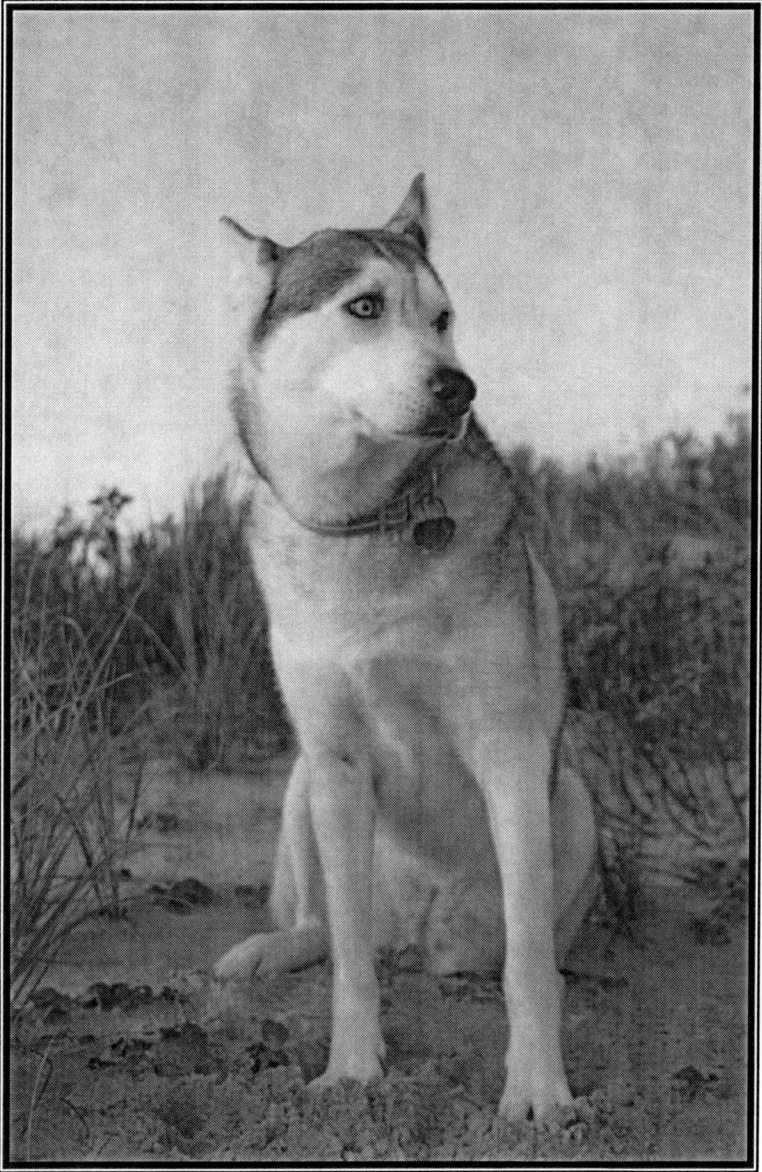

Chapter 1

This is a story about me, Shasta. As you know, dogs can't type, so my friend, Kitchen, is helping me write my story. I am an Alaskan Husky and I love to run! One day, like all huskies down in the lower forty-eights, I want to go to Alaska.

I was born sometime in June 2005 in Tennessee. My mother was abandoned and a stray. While I was still a pup, she was mistaken for a coyote and shot, leaving me all alone without her. Shortly after that, I ended up in an animal shelter. I stayed there a long time.

People would come and go; sometimes, they would take me out and play with me. But I was always afraid of them. The shelter was loud and scary for an orphaned pup like me and I missed my mother. I was still quite young and I wanted her back to protect me from all the other dogs and the strangers at the shelter. But she never came back. I would sometimes give out a long howl, hoping she would respond, but I never heard her.

I began to adapt to life at the shelter, but I was still very scared all the time. People liked me because I was very small for a husky puppy, but they were loud and rough with me. Their kids would chase me and try to pick me up. I didn't like those kids and I began to become very afraid and nervous around children. I don't know how other shelters are run; all I know is that they are not fun places to be, especially for growing puppies. You see, small pups get homes pretty quickly because they're cute, friendly, and small. But once you start to grow, folks tend to ignore you, especially if you have lots of wolf-like characteristics, like I do. People quit looking at me altogether. No one wanted a shy, scared dog that looked and moved like a wolf. The worst part was some folks were actually afraid of me! Can you believe it?

One day a family came by the pound. I tried to act friendly and wag my tail. I pranced around in my cage and yipped excitedly and let out a little howl. The lady glanced at me with a terrified expression on her face and tightened her grip on her kid's hand. I just kept it up, not knowing that I had scared them. The man glanced at me and kicked my cage with his foot. "Shut up, you wolf!" he yelled. I was shocked and quickly fled to the farthest corner of my cage where I whined and cried. I was only doing what the other dogs did to get attention, and the family had been frightened of me! They were talking to one of the shelter workers and angrily pointing at me. "Oh...she's just a husky...not a wolf at all," the worker replied. The family angrily stormed out.

I already told you that I was scared all the time at the shelter. I was so anxious that I wouldn't eat, and I was actually making myself a very sick doggy. Anyway, shelters work like this: they keep you for a while, but if you don't get a home, it's the end of the line for you...they put you to sleep! Every abandoned dog's worst FEAR! My time was just about up, when lo and behold; someone showed up and took me.

Chapter 2

His name was Phil and he worked for a rescue called Second Chance in West Virginia. At this point, I was very thin and very sick. I was afraid, but I was too sick to run away. Besides, Phil seemed like a nice guy. He carried me out to his van because I was too weak to walk.

I was cold and I shouldn't have been; after all, I'm a Husky. But it was because I was so weak from not eating. I also had a bunch of parasites. Phil's van was nice and warm and he talked to me all the way back to West Virginia. He was calm and quiet, and it was nice to hear someone talking to me. No one ever talked to me at the shelter, except to say "Shut up, wolf!" or "Quit that howling!" Phil was the one who gave me my name.

Now, a name is very important to a dog. It lets the dog know she belongs. I didn't have a name until then, and it felt great to have a name of my very own. Phil called me *Shasta* and promised me that he would help me find my very own forever home, which is another thing that every abandoned dog wants more than anything else! We got to the rescue facility, sometime around December 2005. I went right to the vet. Slowly, I started to recover my strength. Eventually, I was well enough to leave Phil's and move to a place called The Yard.

Most animal rescue shelters operate like kennels; the dogs live in individual runs. But at Second

Chance, the dogs all lived together in the Yard. It's a dangerous place, because it caters to a dog's pack dynamics. I couldn't believe Phil was leaving me in the Yard. What did I do? I'd tried to be a good dog. Immediately, I became very afraid of the other dogs.

There was a group of dogs that ran together. They called themselves The Wolves, but they really weren't. The leader was a Golden Retriever mix. I tried to act tough and join them, but I soon realized they were nothing like my ancestors. The Wolves were just bullies always beating up on the weaker dogs and not letting the pups get enough to eat.

I didn't waste any more time with those knuckleheads. I made friends with a lame dog named Baxter. He was bigger, and older than I was and we helped each other out. He became increasingly reliant on me, and the partnership didn't last long.

Because I have very striking wolf-like features, I can appear to be slightly intimidating, a technique I used to my advantage in the Yard. The bullies in the Yard all wanted to be wolves. I looked like one already. The Golden Retriever mix, the Wolves leader, asked me to join his pack. His name was Mel, and I told him, "No, I only fly solo". He was very mad at me and we had a scuffle. Mel was stronger than I was and he cut my leg.

It wasn't serious, but it hurt. After that, I continued to watch out for the Wolves...or as I preferred to call them, the Bullies! They were always guarding the food, making it hard for anyone else to eat. I did my best to sneak food and share with the smaller dogs. I am a wary dog and very nervous. A few times, I got caught and roughed up by Mel and the other bullies. That was life for me: I was still too skinny and I still didn't have a forever home.

Little did I know that was about to change very soon. In February, down in North Carolina, a girl they call Kitchen was searching Petfinder.com for something specific: not just any dog, but an Alaskan Husky. Kitchen had once spent a winter up North, in cold Alaska, on a snowboarding mission trip with YWAM (Youth With a Mission).

It was in Kenny Lake, Alaska, about five to six hours west of Anchorage, that Kitchen's mind was made up. You see, Kitchen met some Alaskan Huskies who took her dog sledding. They were smaller and more muscular than the Siberian husky. They looked more strikingly wolfish, like me. The Alaskan Husky isn't some purebred priss, either. We are strong, tough, working dogs. Kitchen easily fell in love with wild Alaska, so it was no surprise that she would also fall for the energetic, intelligent, and independent-spirited Alaskan Husky.

Now, Kitchen was looking for not only a sled dog, but specifically, a dog that needed to be rescued. She searched for weeks for that special canine. There were other candidates, some closer in North Carolina and others as far away as New Jersey and Georgia. Those other dogs ended up not working out. They all got a home, I am sure, but, they weren't what Kitchen was looking for in a dog.

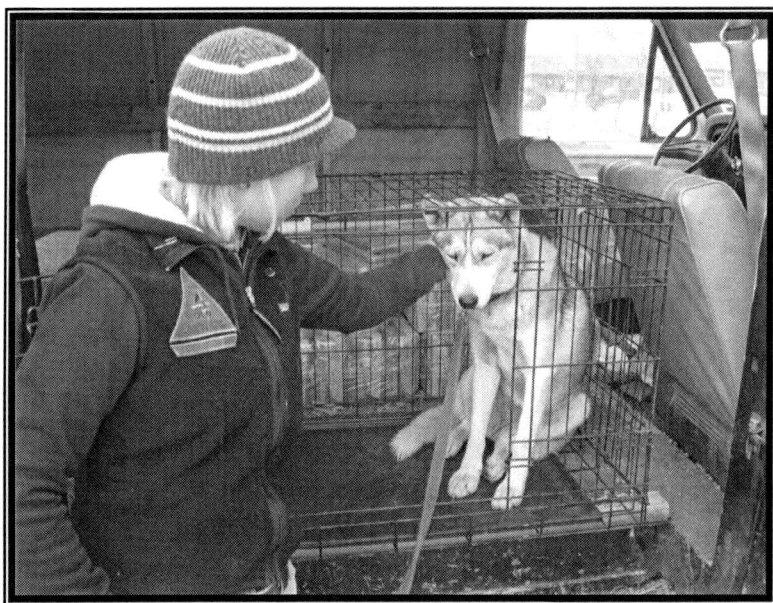

Chapter 3

I remember the day I first met Kitchen and her friend, Tim. Phil came by the Yard and put me on a leash. I assumed we were going to the vet. As I mentioned earlier, I was sick a lot. However, this time we didn't go to the vet. Sometimes we went to Pet Smart or Petco, hoping that the people there would adopt me.

I'd been there several times, but nobody ever showed any interest in a young, half-starved husky. By this time, I had become very shy, especially around kids. At the Yard, the Bullies teased me and said mean things to me like, "Shy Shasta will never find a forever home because she is too shy!" and "Everyone knows humans don't want frightened dogs like you, shy Shasta!" I ignored them for the most part, but it really did hurt my feelings.

Today, Phil was taking me somewhere new. It was a cold and rainy February morning, my kind of weather! I was nervous because I didn't know where we were going. Phil was on the cell phone talking, and every once in a while, he would turn around and smile at me. I was riding in the back of his van, safely in my crate, surrounded by bags of donated doggy chow, which Phil would be taking back to the rescue facility. "Today is a big day for you, little girl," Phil said as we stopped at a light. I didn't know where we were going, so I backed away to the farthest corner of my crate, away from him. "Don't be afraid, Shasta; I'm taking you to meet someone very important!" Phil said. And that is when he started telling me about Kitchen.

Until then, I'd never heard of her. Phil told me Kitchen was a surfer from North Carolina who had just moved there from Virginia. That part I didn't really understand, but then he started talking about hiking, camping, walks, and lots of other outside stuff.

My ears perked up a little bit. Kitchen loved the outdoors and cold weather; she'd even been to Alaska! After hearing that, I lay down in my crate and thought about Kitchen and me racing across the frozen, Alaskan wilderness to bring medicine to kids in Nome! It would be just like great Uncle Togo and his musher, Leonhard Seppala, long ago when the first Iditarod was run! The dream of every Alaskan sled dog is to mush in the Iditarod. Suddenly and abruptly, my dream came to an end as the words of Mel and the other bullies came back into my mind... "Shy Shasta...nobody wants a scaredy-dog!"

Phil pulled into a Sheetz gas station and, about 10 minutes later, a Jeep pulled up next to our van. Tim, Kitchen, and Mary (Kitchen's mom) introduced themselves to Phil. "Well, are you ready to meet Shasta...the husky?" I heard Phil ask Kitchen. "Yes! Most definitely, I've been waiting for this all morning!" she replied. Phil slid open the van door and opened my crate.

He clipped on my leash and handed it to Kitchen. I wanted to be friendly so she'd like me, but I was nervous and afraid, too. "What if she doesn't like me..." was all I could think about. That didn't last long. The weather was cold for humans and it was sleeting.

It was truly a lovely day for a sled dog, but a chilly day for a person. Kitchen was calm and quiet with me.

She and Tim seemed to pick up on my shy manner. She let me sniff her hands and didn't try to jerk me out of the crate, my comfort zone. She stayed on my level and talked to me. To me! Not Phil, or anyone else, just me. That really built up my confidence.

Slowly, I came out of my crate. Then before I realized it, I had hopped out of the crate and the van altogether. But I was still afraid and I tried to hide behind Phil's legs. He just moved out of my way. Kitchen dropped to her knees and said, "Shasta it's ok...come here." She said it quietly and calmly. Everything she said was calm and slow so I could understand it. I really liked her! I liked Tim, too.

After I'd sniffed his hands, Tim gave me an ear rub I will never forget. It was my first one, and oh!...it felt so wonderful! Kitchen's mom was very nice to me, too. She was a little stand-offish at first, but by the end of the visit, she liked me, too. She thought Kitchen was a little crazy when she moved to the beach, but rescuing a dog! That was even crazier! Especially a husky that sheds a lot and that Kitchen, didn't know very well.

I think Kitchen's mom changed her mind once she got to know me. She let me sniff her hands, too, and said..."Oh Shasta! What long legs you have!" I thought, "After all, I am not some little Terrier, I'm an athlete! My long legs let me run faster." I was only 8 months old then, and I hadn't grown into my legs yet, plus I was still very skinny. After that, Kitchen's mom and Phil retreated to the gas station, while Kitchen and Tim stayed outside with me.

They were so careful with me, making sure I didn't step on any broken glass in the parking lot. Kitchen wanted to run around and play with me, but I didn't understand that sort of thing. Having spent all my life as a stray and an unwanted shelter dog, playing wasn't my first impulse. She tried to get me to run around in the grassy area next to the van, but I wouldn't go. I was afraid to venture that far from the van. Finally, I forced myself to trot around a bit.

Everything was going just great. I was even being *friendly*, and I was actually having a good time with Kitchen and Tim! When Phil came back out of the gas station, I wagged my tail and tried to let him know I liked these people. I pranced up to him and then trotted back to Kitchen and sat next to her. I wanted her to know I liked her, too. Kitchen was talking to Phil, and every once in a while, one of them would say my name or look over in my direction. I got a little nervous and jumped back into my crate in the van.

Kitchen shook hands with Phil and handed him a piece of paper. He said he'd be in contact with her about visiting me again very soon, and he said he'd review the papers she had filled out earlier. She rubbed my ears and promised she would be back for me soon, but I didn't understand what she meant. Tim rubbed my ears too. I liked those ear rubs! Then Kitchen pulled my head close to her, so I could look her in the eyes, "Shasta," she said, "I'm going to come back for *you!*" Now, I don't know that much about people, but most of the time people don't look at animals in the eyes. They feel superior to us or something like that. After that, Kitchen, Tim and her mom left me with Phil. I didn't understand what was happening at all.

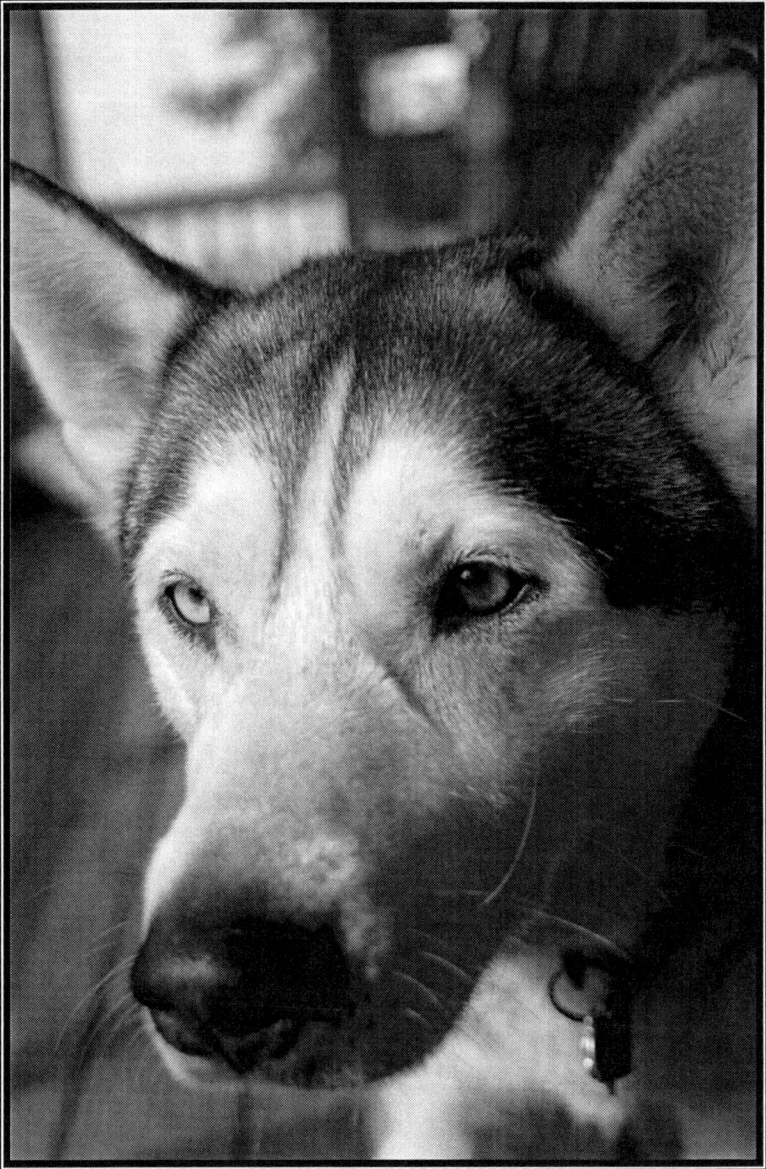

Chapter 4

I thought Kitchen liked me. Why was she leaving? Maybe I should have been more vocal. Just when I thought I'd be getting a forever home, my new family had abandoned me. I was very sad. I curled up in my crate and thought maybe the bullies were right about me. Maybe nobody wanted a shy dog like me.

Phil must have realized I was upset, because when we got back to the Yard, he took me for a nice long walk to cheer me up. It worked a little. I loved walks with Phil, especially when the weather was cold like it was that day. "Shasta, don't be sad; you've got a forever home now, just like I promised," Phil said. "They just need some time to get everything ready for you!"

Kitchen would be back soon to take me on an adventure with her to my new forever home on an island in North Carolina! That made me feel a little better, because I really liked Tim and Kitchen. They were so nice to me. Maybe Phil was right; maybe they would take me back to their island. The "what ifs" had already snuck into my mind, even though Phil promised they would be back. Deep down I doubted it. I trudged slowly back to the Yard.

"Hey, Shasta...how did it go today?" Baxter asked.

"Oh, it went ok, I guess," I sighed, heading off to my dog house.

It rained that night and it was cold. I felt very lonely and I wondered what Kitchen was doing. Was she maybe thinking about me? I decided not to get my hopes up. I let out a long, sad howl, then I curled up and fell asleep.

That night I dreamed about racing sleds, except this dream was different. I was the leader of a team. We'd just gotten to the finish line in Nome, Alaska. The whole time I was running, I hadn't seen my musher. The musher came running around to the front of the team, where I was, and picked me up. "Shasta, my best girl! You won!" It was Kitchen! I yipped and howled excitedly.

She gently put me down. Tim rushed up to me and gave me one of those ear rubs! Oh, it was great! The next morning I felt a lot better. I knew Kitchen would come back for me just like she promised. I stretched and headed out of my dog house,down the hill, towards the old mobile home where the food was.

I wish I could say I had a lovely breakfast; however, it definitely wasn't. By now, the bullies had heard what happened to me and they came over to pick on me. "Good morning, Shy-Shasta! How are you, scaredy dog?!" they said as I walked by on my way to breakfast.

"Don't call me that! I'm more of a wolf than you'll ever be!" I replied.

"Thought you'd get a forever home, huh…Shy-Shasta?" Mel asked, laughing at me.

"I did!…Mel; they'll be back for me in two weeks!" I said, confidently.

"Oh...did Phil give you that lame excuse? That one's more lame than your loser friend, Baxter!" Mel barked.

"Get lost, Mel!" I replied, and headed off for breakfast.

I got into more scuffles than usual with Mel and the Bullies, especially the last week I was in the yard. Thursday, it started to rain, and by Friday, the whole yard was a huge, muddy mess. I don't mind rain or cold weather; I'm an Alaskan Husky, and I have several layers of very dense, lovely, warm fur. It was the mud that was the problem.

I don't mind mud, but the bullies were giving me an extra hard time, because I was leaving the yard the very next day and they were jealous. "They are not going to come for you, Shy-Shasta. You're a mess!" the bullies yelled. My beautiful gray and black fur coat was covered in mud!

"Yes, they will, Mel!" I growled angrily. I'm usually a very mellow dog, but the Bullies had finally pushed me over the edge. Mel jumped at me, trying to make himself the Alpha dog. I jumped back, and he fell in the mud. I quickly moved in, letting him know he wasn't the Alpha dog as far as I was concerned. Two of Mel's pals attacked me on my side. One hit my shoulder, knocking me off Mel; the other took a bite out of my ear.

"Ouch!" I yelped.

"That's what you get for messing with our pack leader, Mel," the dog who bit me barked. I got up and bristled my fur and growled, showing my fangs. I never would have hurt them. I was just trying to scare them. It worked perfectly... maybe too perfectly. Mel and his pack of bullies took off running and threatening to bark about me to Phil. They hollered, "We're gonna' tell Phil you attacked us, Shasta; then those people won't want you!" That scared me. What if they were right? I decided to ignore them. What did they know? Anyway, tomorrow I'd be outta here.

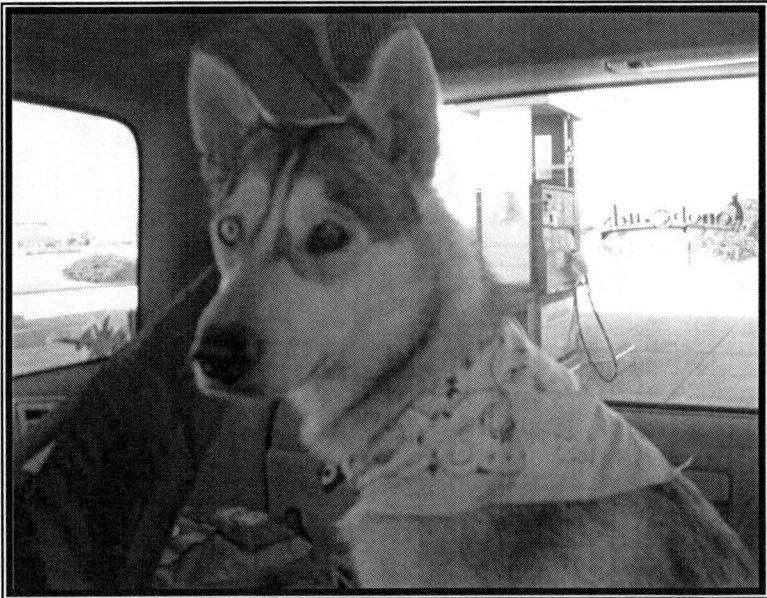

Chapter 5

Finally, it was Saturday... the day I'd been waiting for so long. The day every abandoned dog dreams about! And, finally, it was here: the day Kitchen and Tim would come back for me and take me to my forever home. I should have been excited, but I wasn't. " What if something went wrong and they didn't come, or they decided they didn't like me anymore?" I thought. My ear was still hurting from where Mel's buddy bit me.

Early Saturday morning, Phil came to the Yard and picked me up. As he came towards me, I saw Mel trot over to him. "Probably telling Phil I'd tried to attack him," I thought. Phil just ignored him and headed towards me. He clipped the leash onto my collar and said, "Come on, Shasta, it's time to go to your new home." I hopped into the van and off we went.

It was late morning when we arrived at the gas station. Kitchen and Tim showed up a little while later. I'll never forget it. I was excited and scared at the same time; after all, it had been about two weeks. What if Kitchen had changed her mind? What if she realized that I could never be trusted off leash? I was getting more and more nervous in the back of the van. Phil was outside talking to Kitchen and Tim. Finally, he opened up the back of the van and let me out. I was afraid, and it actually took a lot of work to get me out of the van. I was scared, and I was also covered in mud, which made me feel a little embarrassed. I'd intended to look my best when Kitchen came back for me. Now I was covered in dirt and muck. "It rained a lot this past week," Phil said. I think he was a little nervous, too; Kitchen might second guess taking me because of the mud. She didn't, of course.

She held out her hand towards me, so I could sniff it. I remembered her and I wanted to wag my tail, but I was too nervous. I was so upset I couldn't even jump into Kitchen's 4Runner. (Normally, it is a snap jumping in and out of cars or trucks, but everything was happening very quickly, and I am a nervous dog anyway.) Phil gently picked me up and put me in the metal cage that Kitchen brought for me to ride in, so I'd be safe on the highway.

Just like that, I was off to my new forever home with Kitchen! There was a towel and a big rawhide chewy in the crate for me, as well as some doggy treats, which I didn't like. The chewy was great! I had never had anything like it before.

Once I relaxed a little bit, I began chewing on it. Kitchen talked to me the whole way back. Not about anything really important, just letting me get used to the way she sounded. They even cracked the windows on the truck so I could get some fresh air. I didn't know where exactly we were going, but I was pretty content just to ride in the back.

I was a muddy mess and I felt awful about it, so I started trying to clean myself up a little. Tim said that I looked like a cat in the back of Kitchen's 4Runner, licking my paws, trying to clean off the mud. Before I even realized it, we'd stopped outside some very large buildings. We were in a very big parking lot. That's when I saw the Petco sign!

Chapter 6

Kitchen and Tim didn't know this, but I'd been to Petco before. Not that particular one, but Second Chance used to take us to Petco to try to get us adopted. I hated it! So much going on! So many different smells! Petco is not fun, especially for a nervous rescue dog like me.

I didn't know what was going on! What if Kitchen and Tim were going to leave me there? Would they do that? They seemed "nice", but they are only humans. I've heard tons of stories from other unwanted pets about nice owners. "Nice" owners who get dogs as puppies, and then sell them down the river for a significant other or a new job! I made up my mind when the truck stopped that I wasn't going to Petco. No way! Not me!

It took a lot of manipulation to get me out of the truck. Tim finally had to pick me up and put me on the ground. I was scared and I cowered next to Kitchen. She tried her best to reassure me, but I wasn't so sure about her. Kitchen and Tim took me into the grooming section of Petco. There was a very large white Poodle in there that barked at me. Obviously, she'd never met a rescue dog. She looked like she was living the "good life".

"Please, be careful with Shasta, we just rescued her today and she is very nervous," Kitchen said to the lady who would be taking care of me. It took about ten minutes just to get me into the grooming area, because

I wanted no part of it! Finally, Kitchen dragged me into the back area where the groomers worked and said, "Don't worry, Shasta, we'll be back soon."

"Well, ok", I thought. "They haven't given me any reason to doubt them yet." So there I was at the groomers. I tried to dodge the bath tub four or five times, but I ended up getting my tail wet anyway. I don't like warm water. It's not that I hate it; I just prefer snow.

But, honestly, that bath felt so good! It was nice to be clean. I mean really clean! I couldn't ever remember feeling so good! It took a long time for the groomer lady to finish with me because I was so nervous, and I have three layers of fur.

Finally, I was done. The question now was…would Kitchen really come back for me? The groomer was so nice she seemed to know I had had a rough time. She gave me a couple of doggy treats, which I refused to eat; obviously, I was too nervous and afraid of the blow dryer.

I curled up in the crate and began to wonder, "What if Kitchen forgot about me? What if she changed her mind? Maybe I was too shy and she thought I didn't like her". It wasn't true; I did like her. I even liked Tim, and I'm usually afraid of men. I was lonely and afraid. I whined a little, but I really wanted to howl so I could let everyone know how awful I felt.

None of the other dogs at the groomers knew how I felt, and how could they? Those dogs all seemed to come from nice, warm homes. They all looked so well-fed and I was a scruffy, under-fed mutt, with a cut on my ear. Some of the other dogs tried to comfort me, but I felt too terrible. I was sure Kitchen had abandoned me, too. I'd only known her a short while, so I didn't recognize her voice when she came back for me. "I'm here for Shasta," she said calmly. The groomer slipped a choke leash around my neck, since I didn't have a collar and brought me up front. "Look how clean she looks!" Kitchen said, grinning at me.

"Yeah, she looks great! I guess there really was a dog under all that mud!" Tim replied. I whined excitedly and wagged my tail.

Kitchen gave me a big hug and told me how great I looked. Then she pulled something out of her pocket. It was a collar...for me! My very own collar, with a tag shaped like a heart, and my very own name on it! Oh, I was so excited. She put the collar around my neck, clipped a leash to it, and we were headed back to her truck.

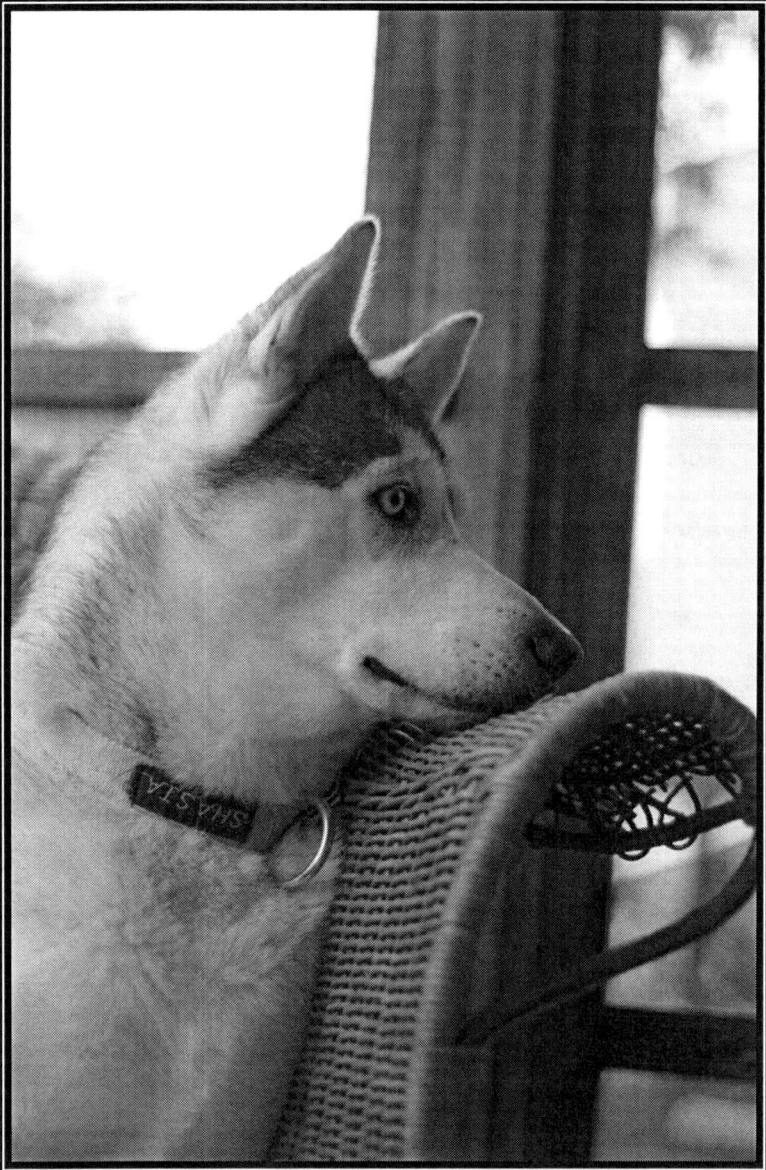

Chapter 7

I was so happy to get away from Petco! Soon we were off again, heading towards Kitchen's parents' house. When we got there, Kitchen's mom was waiting to greet us. "Oh, Shasta! You look so nice and clean!" Mary (Kitchen's mom) said. I wagged my tail and let her pet me. She still thought I had very long legs. Just then, she noticed the cut on my ear.

"Oh, my goodness! What happened to her ear?" she asked, looking at Kitchen.

"Looks like she got into a scuffle," Kitchen replied, carefully examining my sore ear. "We can put some Neosporin on it and it should heal fine," Kitchen said, bending down to scratch my head and carefully rub my ears.

After a walk around the front yard of the house, I was allowed inside! Wow, inside a house! I'd never been inside a real house before! So many new smells, so many new things to look at! Immediately, I smelled dogs.. two of them. What if they were mean and territorial like Mel? Mary must have noticed how nervous I was getting, because she bent down next to me and said, "Shasta, those are my two doggies, but they aren't here. It's ok." Then she carefully pet me so she wouldn't hurt my ear. That made me feel a little better.

For the next several hours, I didn't let Kitchen out of my sight. I even hopped up on the couch next to her. "Shasta! Down!" Mary said, sounding a little annoyed. I quickly hopped down. Clearly, Mary was the Alpha around the house.

"She didn't know any better. Anyways, Velvet is always on the couch," Kitchen replied, coming to my defense.

"Velvet is house broken!" Mary replied, with a little grin.

"Housebroken? What is that?", I wondered. It sounded kind of scary.

Later on that evening, Kitchen put some Neosporin on my sore ear. My ear really did hurt, and I don't think Phil had even noticed it. I wished he had, then I would have ratted out Mel and the other Bullies to him somehow. Mary had noticed it first when I arrived at her house with Tim and Kitchen. "Oh, poor little Shasta!" Mary said, hugging me as Kitchen gently put the medicine on my ear. Mary continued to pet me and she spoke quietly and calmly to me. She told me I was a good dog and that she felt terrible about my ear.

Everything was going ok, when all of a sudden a very loud man walked into the house. "Are we livin' or what!? I'm home!" he shouted. When I heard this, I immediately ran and hid in my crate that Tim had set up in the living room. Who was this crazy man and why was he so loud?

It turned out the loud man was called Ed, and he was Kitchen's dad. He was excited to see me, but I was very afraid of him. I feel bad about it now, but back then, I didn't know any better. I remembered my puppy days in the shelter, and men kicking my cage door and yelling at me to quit howling and crying. I was only howling and crying because I missed my mother. They would've done the same thing if they were me, I bet. From that time on, I kept an eye on Kitchen and followed her everywhere she went. The other eye I kept on that Ed character. I was afraid of him. I did my best to hide behind Kitchen anytime he came near me.

When they sat down at the table to eat, I curled up behind Kitchen's chair, where the Ed character couldn't see me.

I am very nervous around some people, and others don't bother me as much. Kitchen? I liked her almost instantly because she talked to me. She seemed to know I was in trouble. She was always calm and relaxed around me. I liked Tim almost at once, too, mostly because of those wonderful ear rubs which have become his trademark!

Also, he is gentle and quiet to me. Most of the men I have met, aside from Phil, were loud and their voices were harsh and cruel sounding. I was afraid of them. However, Tim was different. I could tell by the ear rubs that he was not a threatening sort of person at all, maybe that was why I first decided to trust him.

Chapter 8

I thought that night would go by uneventfully; however, just as I was settling down, people began showing up. There was a rather intimidating guy name Rob, and later came Ben and two girls whom I liked at once. Not Ben, but the girls. They were very nice to me. It wasn't that I didn't like Rob or Ben, I was just afraid of them.

My mother told me to just avoid things that frighten me, because that's what wolves do. She didn't trust people at all, because the people who owned her were mean to her, so she ran away from them. "Wolves avoid people because they're afraid of them...so never trust a human, my dear one," my mother told me, and I believed her, too. That is, until I met Kitchen and Tim.

It was clear to me that Rob and Ben were there to help Kitchen and Tim move furniture. The weather was still cold and rainy that evening when the guys and Kitchen started moving furniture into the truck parked in the driveway. I had to stay in the house with Valerie and Victoria, the two girls. They were nice to me and I liked them, but I was afraid.

All the loud noises involved with moving boxes and furniture upset me, and I hid in my crate. Worst of all, in the commotion, I lost sight of Kitchen. She disappeared through the door to the garage, where I wasn't allowed to go! I didn't know what was happening. I started to whine, just a little bit at first. I came out of my crate and searched around the rooms for Kitchen, thinking she might have come back through a different door, but I couldn't find her. "Shasta...come here, little girl," Valerie said, looking in my direction. I glanced at her, but I didn't want to go; I wanted to find Kitchen. I didn't want to go sit with the girls and be petted. Well, maybe I did a little bit, but not enough to go back to them. After all, they were strangers to me. Then Victoria said, "Come here, little Shasta; it's ok," she smiled at me, but I just looked at her and whined. Then I hurriedly rushed past them into the safety of my crate.

I sat in my crate staring at the door Kitchen had gone out of, and every once in a while glancing warily at Valerie and Victoria. I continued to whine and cry until, finally, one of the girls went through the door and came back a few moments later with Kitchen. When I saw her, I stood up in my crate and wagged my tail and whined excitedly. I pawed the outside of the crate, but I was too nervous to venture outside of it. "Shasta, come here," Kitchen said, looking at me. I wanted to go over to her, but I was afraid. I yipped and pawed the floor again. "Come, Shasta," Kitchen said again, and this time I didn't hesitate.

I trotted cautiously towards Kitchen who immediately gave me a big hug and told me what a good dog I was for coming to her. Kitchen sat with me on the living room floor and rubbed my ears. She told me I was a good dog and promised me that from here on out, life was going to be a lot better for me. I wasn't sure I believed her then, but I really wanted to. I'd never really known any people before. I'd only known that my mother said that you can't trust them.

However, I felt maybe this time, with Kitchen and Tim, things would be different. "Things will be better," I thought to myself as I curled up next to Kitchen. She was talking to me; I couldn't really understand what she was saying, but I liked the way she sounded.

I was just about to doze off when Tim walked in followed by the other guys, Ben and Loud Rob! Oh, I was terrified! They were laughing and joking. I wished they would go away. The guys really wanted to pet me, but I was afraid of them, so I tried to hide from them. I was shaking with fear; Kitchen put her hand on my shoulder as I sat staring at Ben and Rob. "It's ok, little Shasta. They just want to pet you," she said quietly.

Finally, I let them pet me. They said I had beautiful eyes and they wished I wasn't so afraid of them. By this time, I wasn't as nervous around Victoria and Valerie. I let them both pet me and even hug me too.

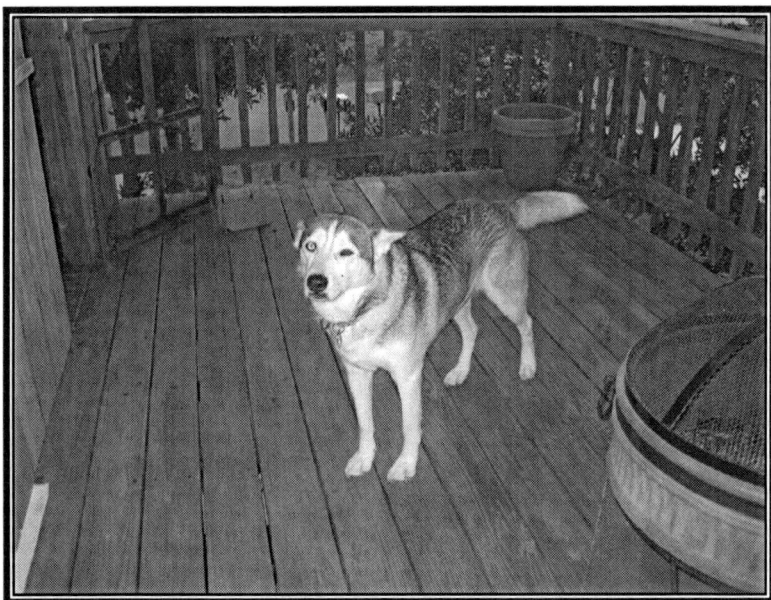

Chapter 9

After a few hours, all the moving was finished, and everyone went home. The house quieted down. Tim sat on the floor petting me and telling me what a good dog I was. Kitchen put some more medicine on my sore ear and then we went for a walk.

It'd been a while since I'd "gone", and with all the excitement, Kitchen thought I might need to go out. I sniffed the whole yard before coming inside a few minutes later. The night was chilly and it had started raining again.

Kitchen said she would have liked to have taken me on a longer walk, but the cold wet weather aggravated her knee. I didn't quite understand that. I love the cold weather, but by that time I was pretty exhausted.

This certainly had been a big day for me, just like Phil had said. In a matter of hours, Second Chance Rescue, Mel and the bullies, everything I'd known before, was gone! No more cold, moldy, plastic crate outside in the Yard! Tonight I was enjoying a treat I hadn't had since I left the pound in Tennessee.. sleeping inside..even though it was in my crate. Kitchen put a nice soft pillow in the crate and camped out next to me, so I wouldn't get scared because I was in a strange place.

The next morning, it was still cold and gray out. Kitchen took me for a nice walk outside. I was enjoying my morning stroll when a truck pulled into the driveway. Out of the truck came that Ed character! "Hidey ho! I'm home!" he yelled to Kitchen. I think the whole neighborhood heard him!

"Oh, hi there, Shasta!" he shouted happily. But he was very loud, and I was so afraid of the loud noises that I had an accident! Luckily, it was on the front walk outside. It was so embarrassing!

"Oh Dad, you scared her!" Kitchen said, laughing.

"Sorry, Shasta!" he said, whispering, so he wouldn't frighten me again. I hid behind Kitchen.

The rest of the day I spent riding in Kitchen's truck. We visited the town of Culpeper. It was very nerve-wracking for me. After we got back to Kitchen's parents' house, I crawled into my crate and slept the rest of the afternoon. I was starting to adjust to Kitchen's parents' house.

I had been very good, according to Mary, because I hadn't left any "presents" in the house. "Presents?" I don't really know what she meant by that, but I guess she doesn't like "presents". Everything was fine that night. Kitchen and Tim took me for a walk around the neighborhood. They talked to me and told me about the Outer Banks. Tim even pointed out the Big Dipper and the North Star. It was wonderful! I could have howled with delight, but I didn't want to scare them. I've heard that people are afraid of wolves when they howl. I didn't know if Kitchen and Tim were afraid of wolves, too.

When I came back from the walk, Mary said since I hadn't left any "presents" on the floors, I could sleep upstairs with Kitchen, in my crate, of course. So I did. The stairs were a bit tricky at first, but I soon mastered running up and down them with no problem. After sniffing around the room, I curled up in my crate. Kitchen sat next to me and scratched my ears as I drifted off to sleep.

Chapter 10

The next morning I woke up and yipped a little at Kitchen. "Come on! Wake up...I have to GO OUT!" She didn't hear me. I barked a bit louder and that did the trick "Out?" she mumbled, rolling out of her bed and onto the floor. Kitchen is not a morning person.

We made it to the front yard just in time...what a relief! We went back inside for breakfast and found out Tim and Ed had gone to Culpeper, and that we were leaving for North Carolina once they got back.

After a breakfast of Ol'Roy dog food (yuck!), which I didn't eat much of, Kitchen took me out for a longer walk. It was still cold, but at least it looked like it would be sunny. We came back inside after our walk and Kitchen gave me a doggy biscuit...(delicious!).

Everything was just fine until Kitchen went back upstairs and left me with Mary. Oh, I was very upset! I didn't know where Kitchen went! I searched all over the house for her. Finally, I let out a sad howl. Mary said, "Oh, Shasta, she'll be right back," but I was too upset to listen to her. I ran up the stairs and noticed one of the doors closed. I howled at the door, because I knew Kitchen was behind it. I could smell her from under the door. I paced around upstairs and discovered the guest room.

Then, I left Mary a "present" in the guest room... not on purpose. I was just scared and nervous. I felt awful about it, but I wasn't quite house-broken yet. Kitchen came out of the door about five minutes later. I was very happy to see her and she told me she'd heard me howling and that she thought I had a lovely voice. She also mentioned something about a shower, but I ignored that part. I was just glad she was back. "Whoa…!" Kitchen yelled, stopping in her tracks outside the guest room door, gawking in horror at the "present" I'd left. That was kind of a messy ordeal, but Mary wasn't that upset. She decided it was my nerves and that I was just scared. She made Kitchen clean it up while she took me out for a short walk.

Tim and Ed came home later that morning and we were soon on our way to the Outer Banks, my new home. I rode in Kitchen's truck with Kitchen and Mary. Thankfully, Ed drove his own car and Tim drove the U-haul.

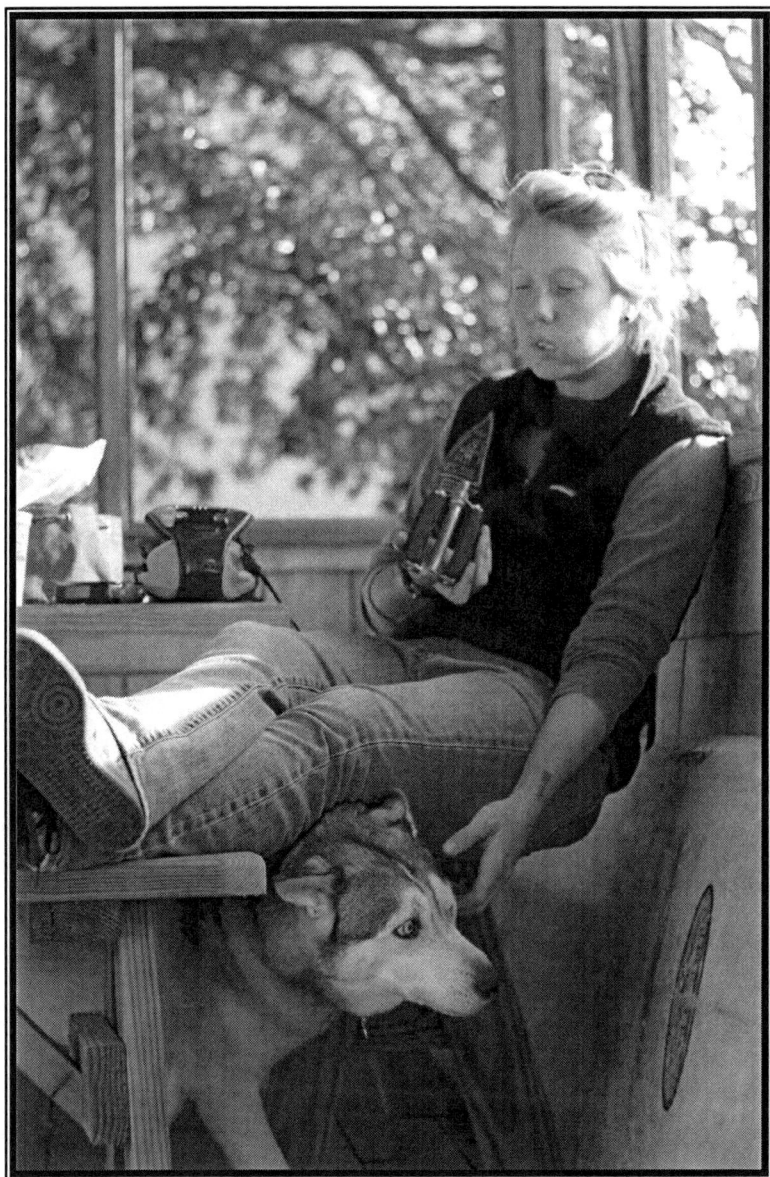

Chapter 11

It was a very long car ride, but I had had the biggest weekend of my life. I slept most of the trip. Of course, at first, I was nervous. What if they decided they didn't want me? What if we weren't going to my new forever home? What if Kitchen was taking me back...to Second Chance! Horrible thoughts crossed my mind. I tried to shut them out. I whined a little and glanced around uneasily at Kitchen.

"What's wrong, little Shasta?" she asked, reaching back to give me some reassuring pets. "Oh, what a good girl you are, Shasta," she said rubbing, my ears. Aah! it was just what I needed. I settled back down and continued to doze the rest of the way.

Finally, we stopped at a gas station. "Oh, no!" I thought. I'd been dreading this the whole trip. Were they going to meet Phil here? I had tried to be a good dog, but maybe I just wasn't right for Kitchen. I whined and paced around the back of the 4Runner nervously. Kitchen clipped my leash to the new collar she'd given me. I didn't want to get out of the truck; I was afraid.

"Come on, Shasta, it's ok; we're going for a walk. It's been a long ride."

"A walk!? A walk where!? To Phil's van?" I thought. "No way! I don't want to go back there!"

"Come on Shasta", Kitchen said quietly. "Just right over there in the grass." Slowly, I glanced in the direction she was pointing. I didn't see Phil's van, just a small patch of grass. It seemed safe enough. Cautiously, I jumped out of the 4Runner and walked slowly towards the grass. Oh, what a relief! I really did need a good walk. After walking around and stretching my legs, I saw Tim next to the U-haul. We walked over so I could say hello. I jumped right up next to him in the U-haul and wagged my tail. He smiled and gave me lots of pets and one of his famous ear rubs. "What a life! A dog could really get used to this," I thought, as I jumped back into the 4Runner.

When I woke up next, we'd arrived at the house on Franklin Street in Kill Devil Hills. Mary and Kitchen took me for a nice long walk around the neighborhood. Then we unpacked all the stuff in the U-haul. It was more a Tim and Ed job. Kitchen, Mary and I organized everything and put some of it away. This was more Kitchen and Mary, but I was there for moral support.

Finally, everything was unloaded and the U-haul returned. Kitchen filled up my dish up with dog food.

"No, I don't like this. Yuck! It's horrible!" Obviously, Kitchen has never eaten dog food! I've tried just about every brand there is. Shelters get a lot of donations in the dog food department. I ate some if it anyway, even though it was just awful!

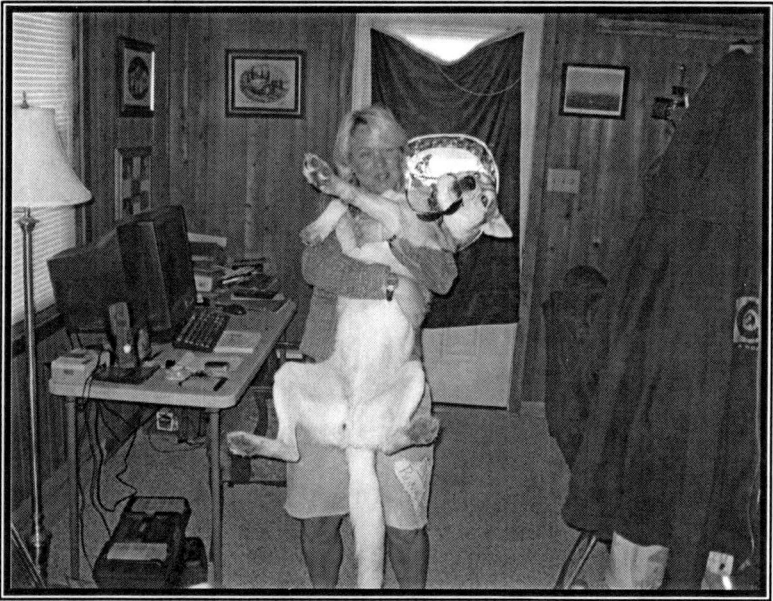

Chapter 12

As I mentioned earlier, I wasn't quite house trained. Because of that slight imperfection, I had to stay in my crate when my people weren't home. This might have bothered some dogs, but not me. My crate was like my safe zone…my den.

It was my own space to curl up for a nap or to hide from strangers. Most folks think a dog crate is cruel, and maybe some people take advantage of crates. To me, my crate was an escape, my own space.

Kitchen had placed a nice soft blanket in the crate for me to lie on. She also set it up in the living room. After a walk around the neighborhood with Tim, I went back up the stairs into the house. Mary and Ed were hungry, and Kitchen agreed that it was definitely dinner time. She also said that "Eight Below" was playing at the movie house. "Oh, Eight Below"!" Mary said, giving me a few very nice pets. "Let's go see it!" she remarked, smiling at me.

"Do you think Shasta will be ok?" Kitchen asked, giving me a concerned glance.

"Yep, she'll be fine. Plus the movie doesn't start until eight, so we can come back and check on her after dinner," Tim said.

"Alright …come on, Shasta, get in your crate," Kitchen said. I got up and walked into my crate, stretched a bit and then laid down. Kitchen knelt in front of me and rubbed my ears. "Oh, Shasta. Be a good dog!" she said quietly, so only I could hear. I yawned and licked her face. I knew they were going out for awhile, but I was sure they'd be back. Kitchen closed the door on my crate, left the light on, and locked the door to the house. I heard the truck pull out and head down the street.

They'll be back. I'll just take a nap, and when I get up, they'll probably be here. I tried to take a nap but I was too upset. I gave a few howls and waited for a response. Then I really got nervous. What if they'd abandoned me here in this house alone! What if they were lost? People get lost a lot easier then dogs do.

The "what ifs" made me anxious and my anxiety began to get the best of me. I realized I had to get out of my crate. Just as I was coming to my breaking point, I heard the truck pull into the driveway; they were back! Tim took me out again for a short walk and then back inside. Kitchen tried to get me to eat some more dog food, but I wouldn't; it was horrible stuff!

Just before 8 o'clock, they headed back out again. This time I knew they'd be back. I was sure I could just relax. I was awfully tired, anyhow. Kitchen hugged me and promised me they'd be back soon. I buried my head in her shoulder, acknowledging that they were leaving. I wanted to whine, but I was afraid. Maybe Kitchen wanted a dog that wasn't such a whiny baby. Kitchen gave me a few more pets before she followed Mary, Ed, and Tim out the door.

"Just stay calm", I told myself over and over again. I just couldn't relax; I paced around my crate glancing at the door. I figured I could get it open if I really wanted to. I'm an Alaskan Husky, so naturally I'm clever, not to mention a bit of an escape artist. I began digging around the floor of the crate. In the process, I destroyed the blanket that Kitchen had put in the crate for me.

I needed to get out of that crate! I couldn't see out the windows. I seriously began to panic! Pushing my head against the crate door, I realized I could force it open at the bottom. "That's the ticket", I thought. I continued to force the door with all my might. Finally, I had just enough of a space to slither through.

It was a good thing. I was only 35 pounds and a bit too thin. There is no way anything bigger than me could have managed that tight squeeze. My sore ear hurt for a moment or two as I ripped the scab off escaping from my crate. "Freedom!" I howled, scoping out the living room. "Now for the windows", I thought.

The blinds were drawn, so I couldn't see out. They were ugly blinds and they had to go, I decided. So I set about redecorating, like a doggie Martha Stewart. The first thing to go, of course, were the blinds on the side door. The side door has windows that face the deck and the stairs to the carport. "Augh, nuts," I whined, realizing after the blinds had collapsed around me, that if I wanted to look out the windows on the side door, I'd have to spend the entire evening standing on my back legs. "Hmm...what would Martha do?" I thought. "Yes, perfect! Those tacky blinds on the front door. Oh so ugly!" I decided they had to go, too. So I grabbed them in my mouth and gave a good strong tug and down they came! Well, only about half of them fell down. That was ok, though. Now I could see out the front door better. This redecorating had taken me the better part of an hour, and I was exhausted.

Satisfied I could see out the big window in the front door, I trotted over to my water bowl for a drink. Then I stretched, glancing around for a cozy place to curl up. The couch looked perfect, so I hopped up, curled myself into a husky ball, and was soon fast asleep.

I awoke, slightly startled, to hear the truck pull into the carport, followed by feet coming up the stairs. Was it Kitchen coming back? Oh, I hoped so! I yipped and howled excitedly, racing around the living room. Tim unlocked the door and surveyed the damage. "Looks like Shasta did some redecorating," said Mary. Kitchen looked at the crate, noticing instantly the blood from my ear on the remains of the blanket. "Shasta...come!" she called. I could tell she was slightly upset. "Oh, what if she didn't like my redecorating job?" I thought as I trotted towards her. My head low and my tail down, I let her know I was sorry. When I got to her, Kitchen gave me a hug and looked at my ear.

"Oh, I'm sorry, but I couldn't see out the door and I was anxious in my crate," I whined. "Oh, poor Shasta..." Kitchen said, continuing to pet me and looking me over to make sure I wasn't hurt. Tim was a little upset, but he didn't really like the blinds, either. They determined I had cut my ear escaping from my crate. Mary put some more Neosporin on my ear and gave me a treat. I took a few bites, but I was still too upset to enjoy it. Tim took me for a really nice walk and assured me he wasn't mad at me for redecorating.

Over the course of the next couple of weeks I, began to adjust to my new life with Kitchen. She took me out for walks in the mornings, and on her days off we went everywhere together.

There are tons of fancy pet shops on the Outer Banks and we visited them all. We also visited the vet! Not at all one of my favorite places to go! But I kept refusing to eat that dog food Kitchen had gotten me.

The vet told Kitchen to try feeding me Puppy Chow. Let me tell you, that was some good stuff! Ah…Puppy Chow! As soon as we left the vet, we went to Wal-Mart where Kitchen got me some wonderful Puppy Chow; it even had salmon in it! I love salmon. Most people think only cats like fish, but dogs love fish too!

The Puppy Chow did wonders for me. It made my lovely fur coat softer and it helped me put on some weight. Now, I know what you're thinking. Wouldn't that ruin my girlish figure? Well, my figure was about 35 pounds. Every time I went anywhere with Kitchen, which was a lot, people all felt sorry for me! I didn't need sympathy anymore. I was having the time of my life! I needed to be at least 45 pounds!

Within weeks of moving in with Kitchen, I'd adjusted to life as a house dog. I finally knew what it was to like to have people who cared about me. I mean *really* cared about me. I loved every minute of it, except when I had to be home alone. Then I would still get nervous!

Chapter 13

My first adventure with Kitchen and Tim happened about a week after I moved to the Outer Banks of North Carolina. Kitchen and Tim took me to Salvo, a village south of Kill Devil Kills. It was a cold gray day-- lovely weather, in my opinion. This was a very special adventure for me because it was the first time I got to see the ocean. We were in Salvo to move the remains of Kitchen's stuff out of the house where she used to live. The moving part wasn't very memorable to me; I spent most of it enjoying the chilly day on the porch.

Once all Kitchen's stuff was out of the house, the adventure really began. We headed for a walk, not down the street, but on the beach. Kitchen warned me to stay on the path, so I wouldn't get a cactus in my paw. I didn't know what a cactus was then, but let me tell you, definitely avoid them at all cost!

After a quick walk, we arrived on the beach. The ocean was calm that day and I walked cautiously up to it for a sniff. It smelled delightful-- like salt and fish-- but it was too loud. I didn't like the way it sounded. However, I did manage to stick my front paws in the cold refreshing water. After all, I am not a water dog, I am a snow dog!

Tim, Kitchen, and I played on the beach for the rest of the afternoon. We played "chase Shasta", "run as fast as you can", and "jump out of the dunes". Even

I was exhausted after all that running around and I'm an Alaskan Husky!

Tim likes taking pictures, and he took several pictures of my first visit to the beach and my first encounter with the ocean.

All the playing and walking up and down the beach had made us all very hungry. Unfortunately, we hadn't planned on spending all evening in Salvo, meaning that we had forgotten my dog chow! I was very hungry and I wondered whether or not I would get to eat. Tim went up to Lisa's Pizza, and picked up some dinner for Kitchen and himself, but dogs don't usually eat pizza, so I was a bit worried that maybe they had forgotten about me. I wondered if this sort of thing was common among humans.

I was in the midst of ignoring my growling stomach when I heard Kitchen calling my name.

"Shasta, aren't you hungry?" she asked.

"Oh, yes, I'm starving!" I thought as I headed into the kitchen where they were eating pizza. Kitchen put the pizza box on the floor for me and it was filled with delicious pizza crusts! "Oh, I knew they wouldn't forget me!" I woofed to myself as I gobbled up the pizza crusts and pepperonis Kitchen had picked off her pizza for me. I was so happy and full! It was then I realized something very important, too. I wasn't just an item or an accessory to Kitchen, I was important! I was a member of her pack! She had no intention of allowing me to miss a meal and neither did Tim. I glanced at them appreciatively.

"My very own pack," I thought again, sighing contently.

The weather got progressively worse that evening as Kitchen and I headed back towards Kill Devil Hills. Tim hugged me and gave me an ear rub, reminding me that there would always be pizza crusts if Kitchen forgot to pack my dinner. We both glanced at Kitchen. Tim laughed and I yipped and woofed, which is how I laugh. She just smiled at us; I think she knew we were laughing at her. I licked Tim goodbye, then Kitchen and I headed back towards Kill Devil Hills.

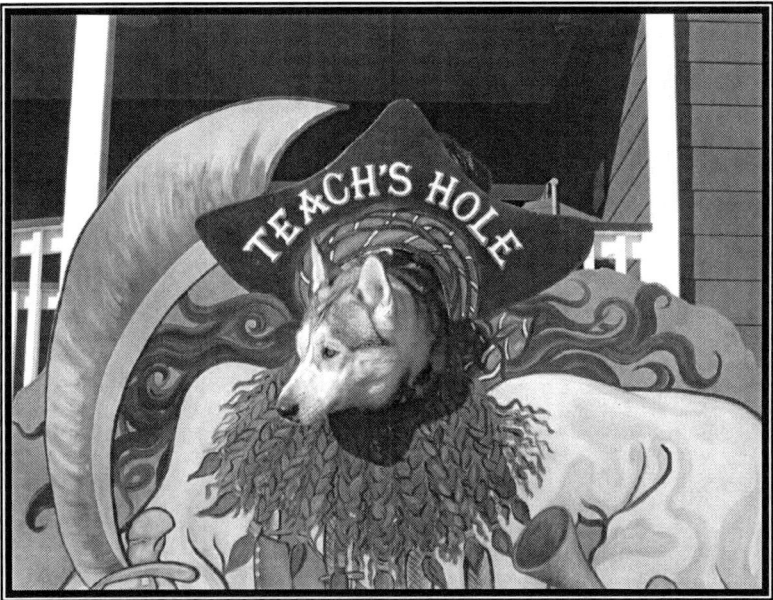

Chapter 14

March was flying by and my memories of life at Second Chance were fading away. One afternoon, we went for a drive to the airport in Virginia. I guarded the car while Tim and Kitchen picked up Jenn and Matthew. Jenn was Kitchen's best human friend from camp. Matthew was Jenn's friend, but I think they were a little more than friends. Well, Jenn was very happy to meet me. I was terrified at first! She talked kinda' funny and she said, "Sha-sta, you're a spag-tak-ular dowg!" I woofed and yipped a little because that's how I laugh. We had lots of adventures on the Outer Banks with Jenn and Matthew.

One day, Jenn, Matthew, Kitchen, and Tim went all the way to Ocracoke on a big boat. Of course, I got to go, too. It was one of the best days ever! We visited the pirate store and I even got my picture taken with my head sticking out of the pirate cut-out! It was a blast! I was so exhausted that I slept all the way back to Kill Devil Hills that night.

After a week of adventures with Jenn and Matthew, the four of them and "yours truly" headed for Virginia again. At first I was nervous. Where were we going I wondered? We drove all day, stopping a few times to walk me, of course. Late that evening, we arrived at Mary and Ed's house.

I remembered them, and I even managed to wag my tail at Ed, assuring him I forgave him for scaring me when we first met. Ed was very happy about that. He loudly announced it to the whole neighborhood as he pet me.

We stayed with Mary and Ed for the night before leaving early the next morning for Pennsylvania. Tim took me out for a long walk and told me that we were going to see Phil on our way to Pennsylvania. Tim told me we would be meeting another dog, and I might soon be getting a brother. I was shocked! I hoped it wasn't Mel! It would be just like him to move in on my family like that.

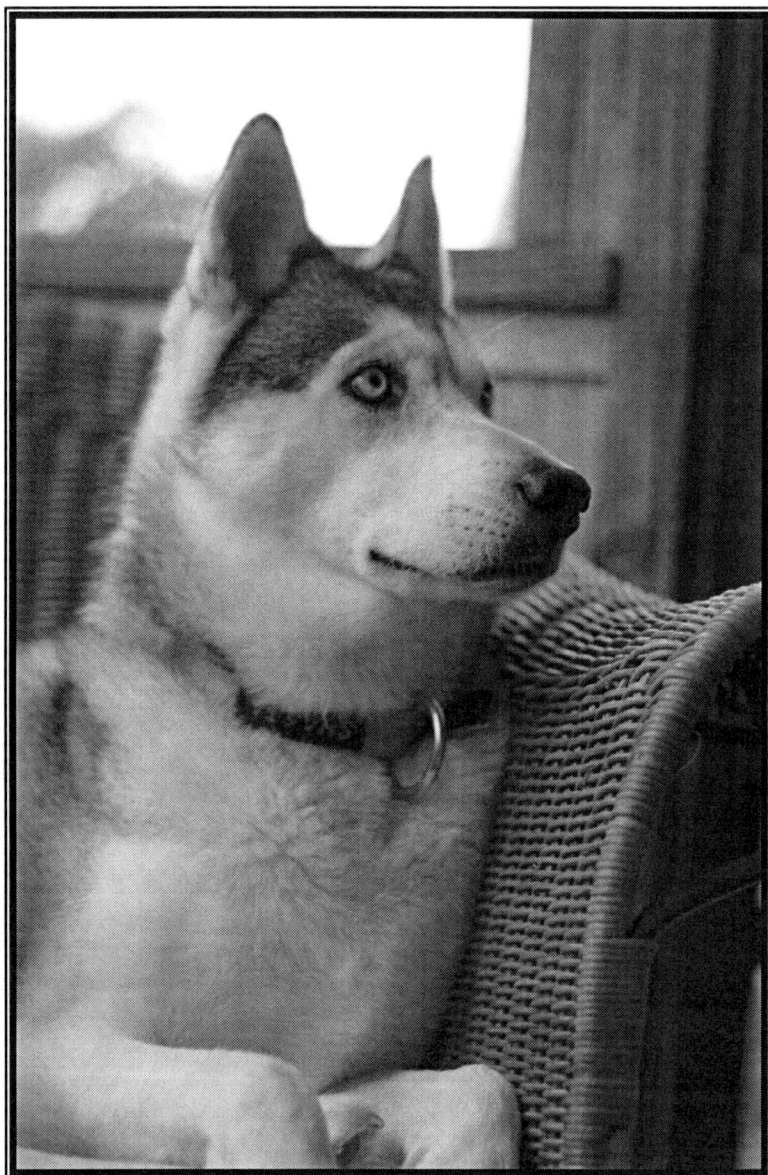

Chapter 15

Several hours later, we arrived at the same gas station where I'd first met Kitchen. Phil thought I looked great. I wagged my tail and I was friendly to him. Despite the poor management and horrible conditions I'd come from, Phil had always been nice to me. After all, if it hadn't been for him, I could have met a cruel and horrible fate at the shelter in Tennessee.

"Shasta, you remember Baxter, don't you, girl?" Phil asked as he handed Baxter's leash to Tim. "Whoa!" I was shocked. I mentioned Baxter earlier, remember? He was lame! A combination of malnutrition and the horrible H-word…Hip Dysplasia, a shelter dog's second, worst fear!

Let me tell you a little bit about Baxter. His rap sheet says he's a Husky shepherd. There wasn't a drop of Husky in the poor guy. He was Akita (I'll explain later) and something else not shepherd. He was also supposed to be about my age-- 8 to 9 months. He was actually about 2 years old.

Ol' Baxter was happy to see me looking so good. I told him he would be Tim's dog, not Kitchen's dog! That position was filled! And if he thought he could weasel in on Kitchen, he'd better think again, because she was *my* girl and I was *her* dog, and we were thick as thieves. But, Tim needed a dog to be a man's dog. A dog's dog! I told Baxter the horror story about Tim being raised by two shih-tzus, and not having a pal to wrestle with and play fetch. Tim tracked around with Baxter who tried to keep up. We spent about thirty to forty-five minutes with Phil and Baxter. Tim arranged to meet Phil on Monday morning to pick Baxter up, much to my surprise. Then we were off to Pennsylvania to visit Tim's parents and the two shih-tzus.

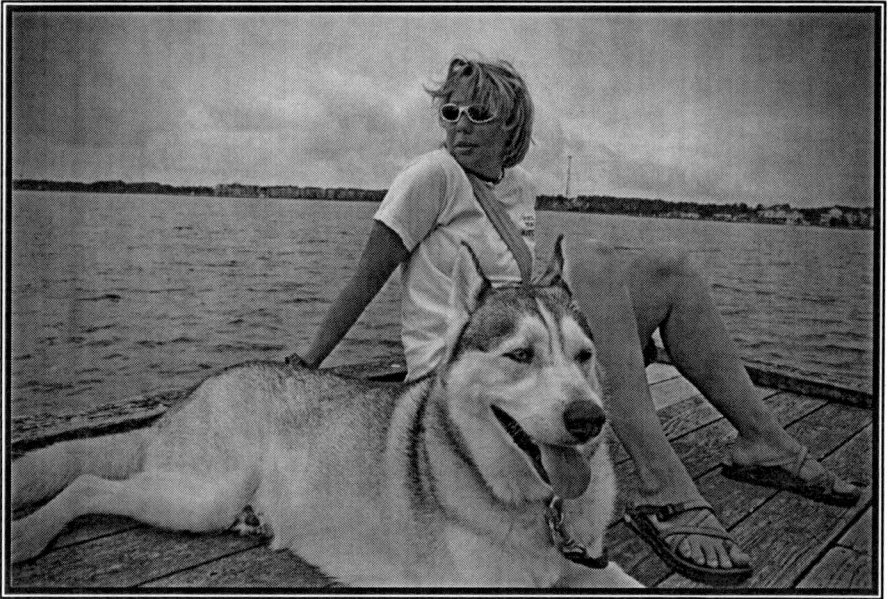

Chapter 16

Well, his parents were very excited to meet me. I was more concerned with the shih-tzus, ha-ha, especially when I realized they were actually real, live dogs. They looked like puppies, and I really wanted to carry them around in my mouth, but Tim said I couldn't. The bigger of the two was completely humorless; he even nipped at me. Nobody yelled at him for it, either. Tim yelled, but he was hushed by his mom who said the dog just acted like that because I was a bigger dog.

"No, I was born bigger than a shih-tzu. I may be an Alaskan Husky, but I am a baby dog," I thought.

I didn't realize he didn't want to be batted in the head by one of my paws. I wanted to stay with Kitchen and Jenn, away from those weird little dogs, but the place they were staying didn't allow pets. I had to settle for staying with Tim, Matthew, and Tim's brother, Dan, at Tim's parents' house. I whined and whined, but finally I fell asleep.

There was a big party in Pennsylvania. That's why we were there. I had to wait in the car during the party, so I don't know what happened inside. I had to wait in Kitchen's 4Runner because they didn't want me to redecorate Tim's parents' house. This was fine with me. I really didn't want be around those two annoying shi-tzus. Tim came out a few times during the party to take me for a walk and I could stretch my long legs. It was nice. We even got to run! Actually, I ran and Tim was on his skateboard. Kitchen bought me a harness a few days before and was teaching me how to run like the dogs in Alaska. She says I am getting good at it. I am having a little trouble turning left. Maybe that's because I am a lefty, like Kitchen. After a late dinner and visiting with Tim's family, I was once again stuck with Tim, Matthew, and Dan.

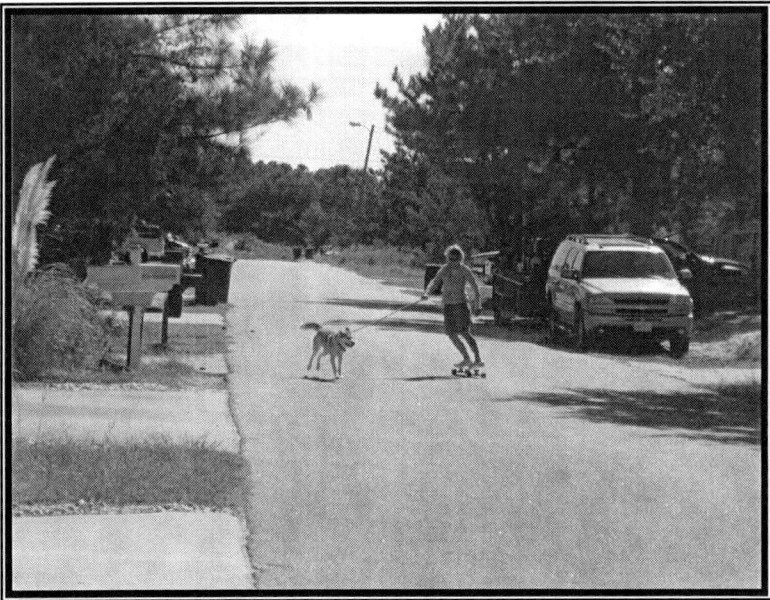

Chapter 17

We left early the next morning. I was glad to be heading home. I liked Tim's parents, but I was very nervous around their dogs. I could never decide whether to play with them or chew on them like toys.

Tim and Matthew picked up Jenn and Kitchen at the hotel where they'd been staying. Then we were on the road again. We drove all morning and into the afternoon before we arrived at the Baltimore Airport. There, we said good bye to Jenn and Matthew. The airport was a busy frightening place, and I was relieved when we were on our way back home again.

Then, it was just the three of us-- Kitchen, myself, and Tim. Tim gave me an ear rub and told me he'd decided to bring Baxter back to North Carolina to live with him. "ok, fine, Tim," I thought. As long as Baxter didn't plan on living with Kitchen and me, he could live with Tim all he wanted.

He could even come and visit, but that was as far as I was willing to go with Baxter. I worried about Tim; I didn't think he knew about hip dysplasia. How could I explain it to him? Tim is more fluent in Bark than I would have guessed, but he's only human, after all.

We arrived in Virginia, (but not home, unfortunately), early that evening. It was cool and damp and felt like sleet- not quite cold enough for snow. Tim took me for an extra long walk that evening. He told me all about the party they'd had in

Pennsylvania. He said one day he wouldn't just be my neighbor! I hope he doesn't plan on sleeping in my bed, I thought. I also wondered what he'd do with Baxter. Certainly Tim didn't plan on bringing him, too!?

We got up early the next day. Kitchen took me out for a skateboard run! She skates and I get to run! Oh, I'm so fast! And because I'm an Alaskan Husky, running is one of my favorite things. We took a short skate that morning because we had important things to do. We worked on my gee (right turns) and haw (left turns). I did great at gee, but haw? Well...nobody's perfect!

After a good run and a short brushing, Kitchen pulled a pretty pink bandana out of her backpack. "For me!" I thought. She tied it around my neck and told me I looked so cute. Of course I did! Pink is a great color on me! Mary told me I looked adorable, but she still thought my legs were too long. "That's because I'm so fast, Mary!"

We hopped into the 4Runner and headed back towards West Virginia to meet Phil and pick up Baxter. We met them late that morning and basically repeated the same process of going to Petco that I'd gone through earlier that month! However, Baxter was ever so much more tolerant of the whole ordeal. It took forever for his fur to dry, because believe it or not it, was denser then my fur! It was also much dirtier, obviously!

I was shocked! Baxter was nice, but Tim had to pick him up several times to put him in the truck. Tim had once pried me out of the 4Runner, too, but that was because I was afraid! Then off we went to Mary and Ed's house.

Tim, of course, was excited about his new dog. However, Baxter seemed to lack the same enthusiasm. It was obvious to me. I'd known Baxter since I'd arrived at Second Chance. By that time, he had been at Second Chance longer than most of the other dogs. Baxter even remembered Second Chance before Mel and the bullies!

I'd told him my life story thus far, but whatever had happened to Baxter in the past, he kept it to himself. I'd never had a human companion and I'd desperately wanted one. Even if I hadn't realized it until I'd gotten Kitchen, I just assumed that every unwanted rescue dog feels the same way.

That was not the case with Baxter. He was two years old, probably closer to three and, like I said, suffered from hip dysplasia. Baxter walked, moved, and felt like an old dog. I wanted to play with him, but I knew he wouldn't be able to roughhouse with a pup like me. I wanted him to know how much fun he'd have being Tim's dog.

As I watched Baxter struggle down the stairs to the back yard, I knew there was something wrong. Baxter used to have no problem with stairs. I glanced at Tim, and I pranced over to him and batted him with my paw.

"Come on, Timmy Boy, I'll roughhouse with you," I woofed, wagging my tail. Tim gave me an ear rub and asked me what was up with Baxter.

"It's hip dysplasia, Tim," I huffed, reading Tim's concerned expression as Baxter hobbled inside.

It was a sunny afternoon so we decided to go for a walk. Mary and Ed lived in a big neighborhood with lots of trails to walk on. We headed up the street. I walked slightly ahead of Baxter to let him know I was top dog.

"Baxter, are you OK?" I asked over my shoulder.

"Oh, my legs hurt, Shasta," he groaned. It was the first thing he'd said to me all day! We had gone a short distance from Ed and Mary's house when Baxter collapsed! He groaned, and then his feet gave way under him. "Baxter!" I barked. Tim looked shocked. Kitchen looked at me with a rather stunned expression on her face. I looked back at her with the same expression as I sat down next to her.

"Baxter, get up, come on!" Tim said. Baxter starred up at him with an awful look on his face.

"I want to, but I just can't. I'm so sorry," he whined.

"Is he OK?" Tim asked Kitchen. She looked Baxter over gently, feeling each of his legs. "Nothing is broken," she said, glancing at Tim. Tim tried to help Baxter up, but the poor dog collapsed again. Baxter wouldn't even look at me. It was awful to watch and I was glad when Kitchen took me back to the house. Kitchen said that Tim ended up having to carry Baxter back to the house. That night Tim took me for a walk. I could tell he was feeling kind of down about Baxter.

"What am I going to do, Shasta?" he asked as we walked. I wagged my tail and nudged him with my head.

"Don't worry, Tim," I woofed. After our walk together, I headed up the white stairs to Kitchen's room. Tim had to carry Baxter to the big room downstairs where they stayed.

That Monday, Tim had to go to work in Culpeper. Mary suggested taking Baxter to the vet. Kitchen thought that was a good idea. While we waited for the vet to open, Kitchen was doing some research about what might be the problem with Baxter.

She was looking at Baxter and at pictures on the computer; I knew it was a computer because I had heard Kitchen call it that before. She thought Baxter looked a lot like the Akita breed. She'd read that Akitas could sometimes be aggressive toward other dogs. Kitchen was worried that if she left Baxter and me alone, something bad might happen.

Chapter 18

Once it hit 10:00 a.m., one of the craziest days happened. Tim was off at work and Kitchen took Baxter to the vet. She promised to keep me posted on Baxter's condition. Mary volunteered to spend her afternoon with her favorite Alaskan Husky, me!

Baxter was a little leery about going anywhere with Kitchen, mostly because I'd explained earlier that Kitchen was *my* girl. However, I was in no way threatened when my Kitchen picked up 60 pound Baxter and put him in her truck, since he couldn't get into the truck himself.

She rubbed my head and told me she'd be back soon, and this time I knew she would be. Yes, I was still nervous, but I knew she would come back. I wagged my tail, acknowledging her.

Hours later, I heard the 4Runner pull into the driveway. I yipped excitedly and ran to the front door with Mary following close behind.

"What did the vet say?" Mary asked Kitchen.

"The vet thought it was Lyme disease at first but now he thinks it might be hip dysplasia," Kitchen replied. "I think I should call Tim about this."

"I think so, too," said Mary.

I didn't hear what Kitchen said to Tim. I knew enough about hip dysplasia to get the gist of the conversation. The long and short of it was that they wouldn't be able to keep Baxter. Tim couldn't afford the cost of the meds or surgeries that would become necessary to give Baxter the quality of life he deserved.

It was a sad evening when Tim got home from work. We were supposed to leave for North Carolina, but instead, Tim and Kitchen were taking Baxter back to Phil. It was for the best, Tim and Kitchen told themselves. They were devastated, especially Tim, at having to give up Baxter.

Kitchen told me Baxter was happy to see Phil again, happier than he'd been all weekend with us. I've always felt Baxter was relieved to go back to Second Chance.

Some dogs will do anything for a home, because they know what it's like. Some, like me, have no idea. Now that I know, I never want to go back to the life I had before. I think other dogs are just crushed by the betrayal or abandonment by their former owners. Baxter was like that, I imagine. I don't doubt it was hip dysplasia, but I think it broke his heart to be abandoned, and I doubt he ever recovered.

When Tim and Kitchen came back, I greeted them as solemnly as I could. Tim gave me a huge hug and buried his face in my shoulder.

"It's ok, Tim, you'll find a pal," I promised.

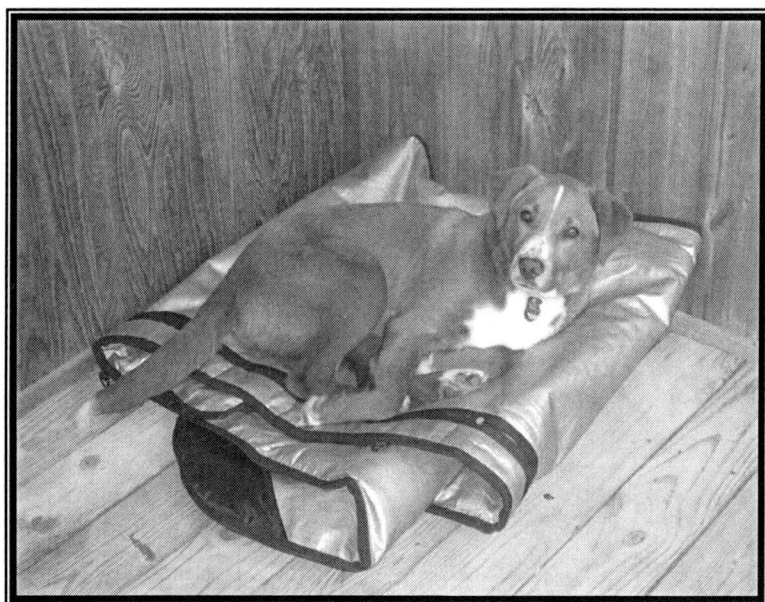

Chapter 19
-The Coming of Denver-

We got home late, and it took Tim even longer, because at the time, he was still living in Salvo, 45 minutes south of us. Kitchen and I were on Petfinder.com the next morning when Tim arrived for work. We talked about it and decided Tim should get a collie dog.

" A Border Collie", I thought, "would be a fun dog for Tim. They're a fountain of inquisitive energy". Kitchen agreed that a ball-fetching collie dog would be a perfect pick-me-up for our little Timmy. Tim liked the idea also. A super-active high energy puppy dog was as different from a shih-tzu as night is from day!

It was Tim who found a 6 month old red puppy dog at the Pitt County SPCA. He called about the pup, and arrangements were made to go on Saturday out to Pitt County, about two hours west of where we live, to meet this dog. Tim didn't want to jump into anything in a hurry, because he was afraid what had happened with Baxter might happen again.

Finally the weekend came! Tim arrived early at the house and picked us up. I was so excited that when we stopped in Nags Head to get coffee, I tried to escape and run all the way there! Tim yelled and Kitchen grabbed me and down we went, tumbling to the ground in the parking lot.

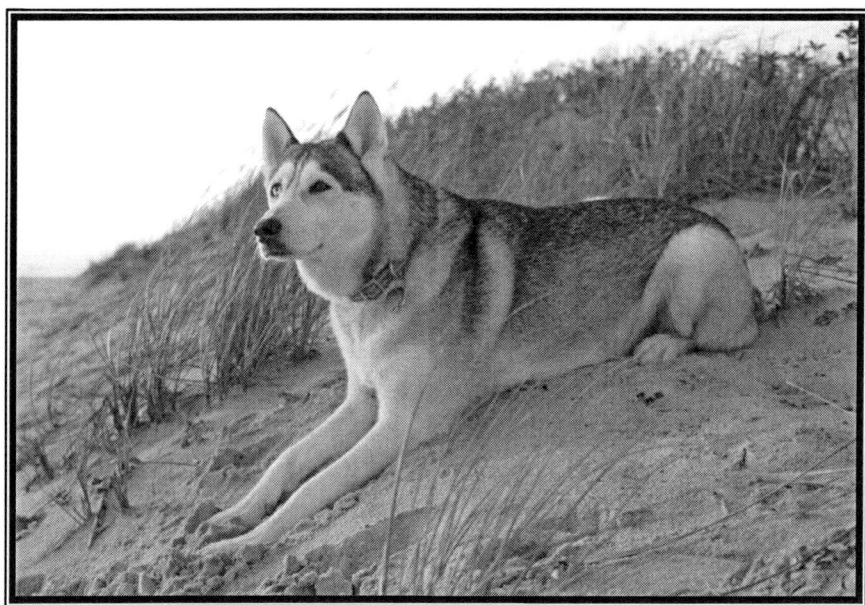

"No! Shasta!" yelled Kitchen, not letting go of me until Tim had my leash clipped to my collar. That's when I noticed the "big road". I could have been killed by oncoming traffic. Kitchen and Tim had saved my life…again, whew! I had no idea how dangerous it was until I saw the oncoming cars!

Tim put me back in the Jeep. After they came back from getting their coffees, I thoroughly apologized by pawing and licking them. Then we were off to the animal shelter to meet a certain little red puppy dog.

We ended up driving by the shelter once or twice. I knew exactly where the shelter was; I could smell it. Alaskan Huskies have a great sense of direction. How do you think we know how to get to Nome, Alaska, for the end of the Great Race? When we finally arrived at the shelter, I decided to wait in the truck. I'm not a big shelter fan. The way I see it, I've spent enough time there.

While they went inside I waited in the Jeep. Kitchen told me about it later. The red puppy was sweet and shy, but very excitable. Judging from that, I'd say he had good ole' Timmy Boy under his paw instantly! I heard he was nervous at first, but he warmed up quickly. Now that puppy captivated Tim, so there was only one thing left to do! What was that, you're wondering? The deciding factor was me, of course! So Tim brought the pup outside, and Kitchen put on my leash on and out of the Jeep I jumped. I wagged my tail happily at the little fella'.

"Hello, little brother!" I yipped.

"Yikes, a wolf!" he whined.

"No, little brother. I'm Shasta. what's your name?" I laughed, barking happily.

"I'm Denver!" he barked. "Ya wanna' be pals?"

I knew Denver would be perfect for Tim. I smiled at Tim and Kitchen and barked my approval of little Denver.

"I think Shasta likes him," said Kitchen.

"I couldn't agree with her more!" Tim replied happily, giving Denver his own first ear rub!

"Oh! that's great!" growled the little dog happily.

"Tell me about it. It just gets better from here!" I yipped.

Tim signed all the paper work for little Denver that very afternoon. It turned out that Denver had been on a list of dogs to work with inmates at the local jail. Instead, he came home with us. I made it clear that Kitchen belonged to *me*. I also told Denver about Tim being raised by the shih-tzus. He thought that was hysterical!

"Well, if Kitchen is *your* girl, Shasta, then Timmy will be *my* boy and I'll teach him to play frisbee and ball and fetch!" yipped Denver excitedly.

"Absolutely! And we'll have adventures, Denver. Lots of them!" I told the little dog. He yawned and curled next to me.

I yawned contently and glanced around. In the course of two months, my life had changed radically for the better! I must be the happiest Alaskan Husky in the lower forty eight states! I've got a girl, a Tim who gives ear rubs, and a new little brother. I don't know what the future will hold, but as long as I've got my new family, I know it will be a great adventure!

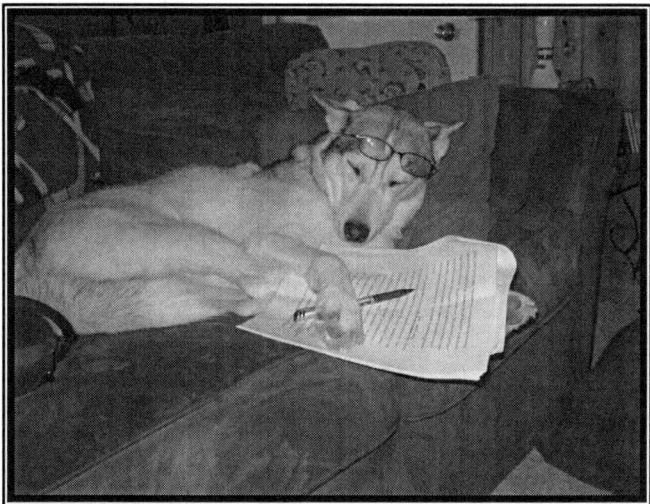

About the Authors: → see updates ✓

Shasta is an Alaskan Husky who lives on the Outer Banks of North Carolina. She was and is the inspiration behind this book. Shasta enjoys camping, hiking, skateboarding, and traveling. Since finding her forever home Shasta and her pal Denver have traveled all over North Carolina and Virginia. Last fall Shasta traveled to Massachusetts and Canada, she of course plans to write about her adventures.

Kitchen has acted as Shasta's hands, writing and correcting Shasta's first book. Kitchen has loved reading books all her life. She was inspired to help Shasta write her book after reading "Roverandom" a book about a brave little dog who has many adventures, written by her favorite author J.R.R. Tolkien. Kitchen enjoys camping, hiking, and anything else involving the great outdoors, especial when she can take her best girl Shasta along with her.

Shasta had a long and happy life! She traveled all over the east coast of the United States and Canada too. The played with her best pal Denver. She loved skateboarding and adventures. In 2018 she passed away peacefully after being sick w/ Cancer. She was surranded by her loving Family.

Lindsey "Kitchen" Kitchen now lives in USK, Wales with her family. Currently she does not have a dog. After Shasta passed away Denver continued on living before he also passed away. ~~the~~ For a brief time the family had a lovely luncher named Vos who died from Vet misdiagnosis before moving to Wales.

Perhaps stories about Vos will soon be written as she was quite a hilarious little dog.

LaVergne, TN USA
16 November 2010

205005LV00001B/1/P